My *30* *Week*
Gratitude Journal

A place to
celebrate the pleasures
experienced every day.

Published by HieroGraphics Books, LLC
First Printing, July 2015
Second Printing, February 2016

Printed in the United States of America

HieroGraphics Books, LLC
https://www.hierographicsbooksllc.com
106 Ruxton Ave
Manitou Springs, CO 80829

ISBN-13: 978-0692671368
ISBN-10: 0692671366

My 30 *Week*
Gratitude Journal

**A place to
celebrate the pleasures
experienced every day
and**
*heart-based images
for you to color.*

Julia L Wright

HieroGraphics Books, LLC

Dec. 25, 2020

Dear Jayde,
    I am so grateful for you and am
so proud of you. I hope this
little book helps you stay
mindful of all your blessings!
                    I love You!
                    Annie

This Gratitude Journal Belongs To:

_____

Related Books Published by HieroGraphics Books LLC

Monthly Dream Journal by Julia L. Wright

Discover Essential Oils for Optimum Health by Julia L. Wright

Gratitude Journal by Julia L. Wright

My Hiking Journal by Julia L. Wright

My Camping Adventures Journal by Julia L. Wright

Handbook To Health
by Vivian Rice and Edie Wogaman
Revised and edited by Julia L. Wright

Where Do I Belong? by Susan Grace

*Galloping Wind: The Legend of Wild Shadow,
The Wind-That-Gallops* by Zoltan Malocsay

Sinister Frog: A Radio Show for Twisted Minds by Bob Kelsey

Natural Health Book Series Based on
Orison Swett Marden's *Cheerfulness As A Life Power*
Available on Kindle, Revised and enhanced by Julia L. Wright

Book 1: Laughter and Essential Oils:
Natural Cures for Dis-Ease

Book 2: Optimism and Essential Oils:
Natural Cures for Depression

Book 3: Positive Attitude and Essential Oils:
Natural Ways to Alleviate Stress

Book 4: Cheerfulness and Essential Oils:
Natural Ways to Create a Joyful Life

Book 5: Giving and Essential Oils:
Naturally Create the Life You Desire

Book 6: A Sunny Nature and Essential Oils:
Naturally Create Optimum Health

As A Man Thinketh
by James Allen - Revised and enhanced by Julia L. Wright

Download your bonus set of Gratitude Quote Cards created using 36 beautiful photographic images from Julia L Wright, matched with GRATITUDE QUOTES by 36 world renowned positive thinkers.

Sign up to download:
"My 30 Week Gratitude Journal Bonus Quote Cards", at:

www.hierographicsbooksllc.com/quote-cards-gratitude-journal.

The thirty gratitude quotes that begin each week on the following pages are matched with a beautiful image. You can carry each week's quote with you to help keep you on the steps on the path for your new approach to life.

There are six *"bonus"* quote cards to place in various spots around your home or work space to help keep your mind focused on the beautiful and positive things in this world and remind you to express your gratitude for them daily.

For more insights on expressing gratitude, ways to fall asleep naturally, and creating abundance in your life visit:

www.HolisticSteps.com

Table of Contents

Introduction to Gratitude Journaling

Keeping a gratitude journal and expressing gratitude on a daily basis is a simple practice that can change your life in many ways. Writing daily in a *Gratitude Journal* or *Pleasure Book* will shift your mindset to a more positive and joyful approach to your world.

Studies have shown that when people keep gratitude journals for as few as three weeks the results have been overwhelmingly positive.

People who consistently practice gratitude experience beneficial shifts in physical, relational, spiritual and mental areas of their lives. Positive life changing events and improvements begin to occur more frequently in many different areas of their world.

NOW! Imagine how much more effective using this journal for 30 weeks will be for turning your life around for the better!

This *Gratitude Journal* or *Pleasure Book* is the perfect place to write about what you are grateful for having in your life. Keep it next to your bed to reflect on your day and write in each night before going to sleep. You may want to carry it with you to record amazing experiences at the times when they happen in your life.

NOW! is the best time to start counting your blessings by writing in your gratitude journal.

Your first step towards creating a more abundant and peaceful life by living in the moment and expressing gratitude for all you have and experience would be to write in this journal about the many amazing and positive experiences that happen every day in your life. Take a little bit of time every day to note, with gratitude, the positive and pleasurable experiences you enjoy each and every day.

A simple way to start would be to reflect upon your day and write a sentence about at least three things that you enjoyed, found pleasure in or were grateful for having a special person or thing in your day.

You don't have to limit your self to just one sentence to describe your gratitude or a pleasurable experience. If something happened during the day that you were grateful for, you might want to focus on that experience and write a longer note about it.

If you are feeling especially appreciative of someone in your life, write about that person and why you appreciate them in more than one sentence. Consider writing a physical thank-you card to hand or mail to that person. Or take time to send them an email expressing your gratitude for their being in your world.

You may want to use this journal in more than one way.

You might find that you enjoy writing something in it each morning to start your day with a positive and cheery outlook.

Or you may want to carry it with you to make a note when something wonderful and beautiful happens at that exact time.

Some people will keep it by their beds to write in nightly. Using this journal is the perfect way to focus your intention on positive things that you experienced during the day to help you have a night of peaceful sleep.

You may find it useful to put down in writing some positive things to focus upon during your dream time.

If you were especially appreciative of someone in your life or something happened during the day that you were grateful for, you may want to focus on that. You can ask your dreams to guide you to steps to take using this positive experience to lead you towards more good and pleasurable things happening in the future related to that person or experience.

Many wise people have spoken about the benefits of expressing gratitude. Each week starts with one of these quotes. You may notice your heart becoming more filled with joy and love every time you express your gratitude to others or in this journal.

Your attitude can easily color your day and that of those around you. Research has shown that coloring helps you become more peaceful and centered. That is why you will find pages to color in this journal. Every other week ends with a small image based on hearts for you to color.

Alternate weeks end with a picture to meditate upon the joy you find in that image. Perhaps it will remind you of a moment of joy you recently experienced, or need to pursue in the future. Feel free to add some color to these images also.

While many emotions and personality traits are important to everyone's well-being, there is evidence that gratitude may be uniquely important to experiencing good health and a satisfying life.

When you find yourself feeling down in the future you can look back at these pages to remind yourself of all the things that you have in your life to be grateful for and give you pleasure each day.

It Is Your Choice!

There are many ways to look at and move about in the world.

Many people approach their life in the most positive ways and are a joy to be around, while other folks drift through their days and experiences without recognizing or acknowledging all the good things in their lives. And some people have the attitude that *"nothing ever goes right"* for them and are very hard to be around.

Which one are you?

If you have been negative in the past, using this *Gratitude Journal* is the perfect place to start to shift your mindset. It offers you the opportunity to step into a positive and joyful approach, creating a more abundant life for yourself and those you love.

By using this journal, to write about the many amazing and positive experiences that happen in your life, you will be stepping on a path to creating a more amazingly pleasurable and abundant life.

NOW! is the best time to start taking the time to write about the people and experiences that you are grateful for and give you pleasure during each day.

-COLOR ME GRATEFUL-
SYNONYMS AND RELATED WORDS

APPRECIATE

THANKFULNESS

LOVE

PLEASURE

DELIGHTED

APPRECIATION

GRATITUDE

THANKS

GRATEFULLL

ACKNOWLEDGITE

RELATED

OBLIGE

Defining Gratitude

Gratitude, comes from the Latin word *"gratus"*, which means *"thankful, pleasing"* and from medieval Latin *"grātitūdō"*.

Gratitude, thankfulness, gratefulness, or appreciation is a feeling or attitude that is used to acknowledge a benefit or gift that one has received or will receive.

People are expressing gratitude whenever they express a feeling of thankfulness or appreciation for gifts or favors they receive or life's little pleasures they experience each day.

Gratitude means giving thanks and showing appreciation for someone or something in your life. When you feel gratitude, you're pleased by what someone did for you and are pleased by the results.

Expressing your gratitude out loud or in a written note is the perfect way to let someone know of how much they mean to you.

It is the warm feeling you get when you remember the person who complimented your smile or how you looked or suggested using positive words a way for you to make a change that worked to get you back on track with a piece of your life.

The expression of gratitude has historically been a focus of several world religions. It has been considered and researched extensively by various moral philosophers such as Lee Clement. A more systematic study of gratitude within psychology began in 2000.

In the past, psychology had been traditionally focused more on understanding stressful and negative emotions. It rarely explored how positive emotions could affect a person's life. But recently that has shifted. Research has been done that shows how having a positive attitude in life can benefit a person on many levels.

Gratitude, rhymes with *attitude, beatitude, and platitude.* Having an attitude of gratitude during the day can make every day more enjoyable for your and those around you. Others notice when you mention the things you are thankful in your life.

Synonyms and related words are: thankfulness, appreciation, gratefulness, thanks, cite, acknowledge, grateful, appreciate, thank, oblige, acknowledgment.

A   G   W

PLEASURE   R

P   A   FIND

R   G   T   T

E   GRATITUDE

C   A   T   P

I   T   U   L

A   I   D   E

T   T   EXPRESS A

SEE   U   U

X   D   G   R

PLEASURE   E

R   A

E   GRATITUDE

S   I

S S T

H U

O D

WRITE

Creating the Habit of Gratitude

Over the next 30 weeks into your future you will use this *Gratitude Journal* or *Pleasure Book* to write about a variety of positive experiences that happen every day of your life.

There are two pages for each week to express your gratitude in many forms. Use this journal to help you improve your outlook on life. In it you are invited to express your gratitude in many forms in order to assist you in creating a new habit to last a lifetime.

It has been said that when a person adds a new practice into their normal routine and does it for 30 days, it becomes a habit.

Are you ready to create the habit of expressing gratitude on a daily basis to create positive changes to your life?

The habit of expressing gratitude has many benefits.

Take a moment to read through the following list of 30 benefits to better understand how your life can be changed a variety of ways. Then start using this *Gratitude Journal* or *Pleasure Book* to express your gratitude for the many pleasurable and wonderous things you experience and enjoy every day. By doing this you are affirming the good things in your life that you have received from others as well as from your own actions.

Gratitude is a social emotion. It strengthens relationships as it requires you to recognize how you've been supported on many levels by other people. This in turn encourages you to *pay it forwar*d and help others in small or large ways that are within your abilities to change their lives for the better.

Saying *thank you* on a daily basis to friends, co-workers, your spiritual source and yourself acknowledges the gifts you have received and gives you a better vision of the abundance in your life. Expressing gratitude allows you to celebrate the present moment and enhances the positive emotions you are feeling.

Writing in a *Gratitude Journal* or *Pleasure Book* reminds you to take the time to savor the good things that you might otherwise have taken for granted or might have missed acknowledging for the full value it added to your day.

When this journal is filled, don't stop there. Be sure you have another one on hand to continue on your path to the holistic, healthy joyful and abundant life that you deserve.

30 Benefits of Gratitude Journaling and Expressing the Pleasures You Experience Daily

1. Grateful people are happier and experience more joy in their lives since expressing gratitude boosts feelings of optimism, joy, pleasure, enthusiasm, and other positive emotions.

2. Grateful people enjoy better, more rewarding social and close personal relationships.

3. Grateful people discover they have a purpose in life.

4. Grateful people are very generous people.

5. Grateful people feel less stressed, have less anxiety and rarely have the challenge of high blood pressure.

6. Grateful people experience less depression by reliving positive moments in their day and life.

7. Grateful people are more willing to forgive others, not hold grudges or stay angry for long periods of time.

8. Grateful people experience a greater feeling of well-being.

9. Grateful people are better able to dismiss or come to terms with experiencing bodily aches and pains.

10. Grateful people have stronger immune systems and are able to heal more quickly.

11. Grateful people know how to accepted a compliment and say *thank you* rather than brushing it aside.

12. Grateful people accept themselves, recognizing all the positive things about themselves.

13. Grateful people are more resilient and able to find many positive ways to cope with and recover from the challenges they experience in life.

14. Grateful people are more willing to ask for help and support from other people when challenged.

15. Grateful people can reinterpret and grow from experiences rather than dwelling on a challenge they have experienced.

16. Grateful people express their appreciation for small things.

17. Grateful people tend to exercise and take care of their health.

18. Grateful people have more control of their personal environments.

19. Grateful people have a positive outlook for the future and don't dwell upon past challenges.

20. Grateful people are willing and able to learn new things.

21. Grateful people are able to experience more personal growth.

22. Grateful people take time to figure out how to deal with a life challenge or challenging person in a calm manner.

23. Grateful people are able to move through any life transitions more easily.

24. Grateful people find it easier to stay healthier, both physically and mentally.

25. Grateful people use positive coping strategies and are less likely to turn to alcohol or drugs when faced with challenging situation in their lives.

26. Grateful people are more likely to face a challenge, rather than avoiding taking steps to handle and resolve it.

27. Grateful people are less likely to put blame on themselves for being in a challenging situation.

28. Grateful people find it easier to fall asleep at night by counting their blessings before going to sleep.

29. Grateful people say thank you to others for even the smallest of acts of kindness received from other people.

30. Grateful people are more compassionate, helpful and altruistic people who believe that the greater good for all is a higher priority than their own.

This revised and enhanced Chapter IV of "Cheerfulness As A Life Power" by Orison Swett Marden is a simple story to encourage you to step on the path of expressing gratitude and acknowledging the pleasure you experience every day.

A PLEASURE BOOK

She is an aged woman, but her face is serene and peaceful, as though trouble had always passed her by. She seemed utterly above the little worries and vexations, which torment the average woman and leave lines of care on faces of so many other people.

Her neighbor, the Fretful Woman, asked her one day the secret of her happiness.

This question made the beautiful old woman's face shine with joy.

"My dear," she said, "I keep *A Pleasure Book.*"

"A what?"

The older woman smiled and repeated, "*A Pleasure Book.*"

Then she gently went on to explain, "Long ago I learned that there is no day so dark and gloomy that it does not contain some ray of light. I have made it one task in my life to write down the little things which mean so much to a woman."

"I have a series of notebooks I have written in for every day of every year since I left school. The notation may be just a little thing: a new dress or scarf, a bird's song, a chat with a friend, the thoughtfulness of my husband, a flower, a book, the scent of a flower I pass by, a walk in the field, a letter, a concert, or a drive in the country. They all go into my most current _Pleasure Book_."

"Sometimes I have read a poem or heard a joyful song that lifted my spirit, so I will add that to a page. And, if I find myself inclined to fret, I read a few pages from one of my books to see what a happy, blessed woman I am. Would you like to see one of my treasures?"

The Fretful Woman nodded a slight tilt of her head and the aged woman handed her one of her _Pleasure Books._

Slowly the peevish, discontented woman turned over the book her friend brought her, reading a little here and there.

One day's entries ran thus: _"Had a pleasant letter from mother. Saw a beautiful lily in a window."_ Another entry stated: _"Found the pin I thought I had lost. Saw such a bright, happy girl on the street."_ Another page read: _"My husband brought some roses in the evening."_

Bits of verse and lines from her daily reading have gone into the _Pleasure Book_ of this world-wise woman, until its pages became a storehouse of truth and beauty.

"Have you found a pleasure to write about for every day?" the Fretful Woman asked.

"For every day," the low voice answered, "I had to make my theory come true, you know."

"Consider this," she asked in a gentle voice. "Who has a right to rob other people of their happiness? If you are not at the moment cheerful, look, speak, act, as if you were. You must always be aware that your attitude can color your day and that of those around you."

"Although I had little money, I had nothing to give but myself," said this woman who had experienced great sorrows, but who bore them cheerfully.

"Early on in my life I formed a resolution never to sadden any one else with my troubles. I have laughed and told jokes when I could have wept. I have always smiled in the face of every misfortune. I have tried never to let anyone go from my presence without a happy word or a bright thought to carry away. And happiness makes happiness. I myself am happier than I should have been had I sat down and bemoaned my fate."

One of the entries the worrisome woman found to read in the *Pleasure Book* was a poem by Ella Wheeler Wilcox:

> 'Tis easy enough to be pleasant,
> When life flows along like a song;
> But the man worth while is the one who will smile
> When everything goes dead wrong;
> For the test of the heart is trouble,
> And it always comes with the years;
> And the smile that is worth the praise of the earth
> Is the smile that comes through tears.

The Fretful Woman ought to have stopped there, but did not.

Next she found the page where it was written *"He died with his hand in mine, and my name upon his lips."*

This entry gave her pause and she looked searchingly at her neighbor's face in wonderment.

The older woman held the belief that life is not given for mourning, but for unselfish service. With that in mind, she expressed this thought to her friend, "How beautiful is it, if our strange earthly sorrows become a blessing to others, through our determination to live and to do for those who need our help."

Take a bit of time to think upon the lesson from this older, peace-filled woman.

A habit of happy thoughts can transform a life filled with challenges into one of harmony and beauty.

The serene optimist is one whose mind has dwelt so long upon the sunny side of life that he/she has acquired a habit of cheerfulness.

It is impossible to overestimate the importance of forming a habit of cheerfulness early in life.

One needs to practice expressing PLEASURE and GRATITUDE as one would practice when learning any new skill.

Imagine if this aged woman was chatting with you now. She would suggest that if you have made a habit of worrying, it is time for you to take the steps to heal it as you would a disease. This stressful habit is definitely something to be overcome, an infirmity that you need to rid yourself of. You need to turn it about by sheer force of will.

NOW! is the time for you to step into a practice of expressing cheerfulness and gratitude on a daily basis.

It isn't the work one does, but worry, fretfulness and friction that are your enemies to be routed. You should not go about your day wearing a gloomy face, but put on a smile and see how that changes your circumstances for the much better.

Talk happiness. The world is sad enough
Without your woes.
No path is wholly rough;
Look for the places that are smooth and clear,
And speak of those who rest the weary ear
Of earth, so hurt by one continuous strain
Of human discontent and grief and pain.

Talk faith. The world is better off without
Your uttered ignorance and morbid doubt.
If you have faith in God, or man, or self,
Say so; if not, push back upon the shelf
Of silence all your thoughts till faith shall come;
No one will grieve because your lips are dumb.

Talk health. The dreary, never-changing tale
Of mortal maladies is worn and stale.
You cannot charm, or interest, or please,
By harping on that minor chord, disease.
Say you are well, or all is well with you.
And God shall hear your words and make them true

- Ella Wheeler Wilcox

What If . . .
Gratitude Journaling Will Shift Your World

What If . . .
. . . you started each day by giving thanks?
. . . you found a pleasure or two or three every day?
. . . you smiled at a stranger walking down the street?
. . . you expressed your gratitude for being able to walk?
. . . you hugged a friend just because they were near you?
. . . you were grateful for everything in your world all the time?
. . . you said "thank you" to someone for just for being in your life?
. . . you gratefully accepted a compliment without downplaying it?
. . . you told a stranger how much you enjoyed seeing their garden?
. . . you looked in the mirror and told your reflection "I love you"?
. . . you appreciated a farmer for the food he grew for you to eat?
. . . you thanked the rain for nourishing all the plants it touches?
. . . you expressed your gratitude for just being alive out loud?
. . . you told someone how happy you are they are in your life?
. . . you found pleasure in the smallest things in your world?
. . . you stopped and smelled a flower you were passing by?
. . . you appreciated the rain for nourishing the flowers?
. . . you expressed your joy at being alive all the time?
. . . you thanked a bee for pollinating the flowers?
. . . you told a bird you were enjoying its song?
. . . you thanked the sun for shining on you?
. . . you ended each day by giving thanks?

(fill in the blank)

. . . you _____

. . . you _____

. . . you _____

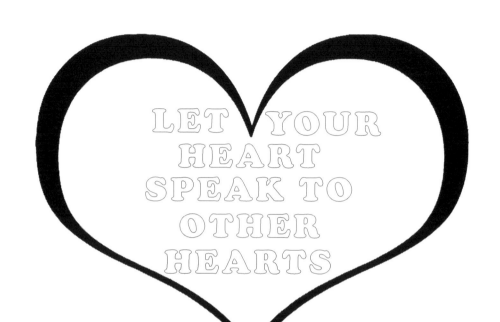

LET YOUR
HEART
SPEAK TO
OTHER
HEARTS

By now You should better understand how expressing gratitude on a daily basis can bring more joy and abundance into your life.

Are you ready to begin your journey into a more pleasurable personal world?

Do you see clearly how a positive, cheerful attitude towards your world can assist you in creating a healthier you?

It is said when you do something for 30 days, it becomes a habit.

This journal gives you the opportunity to daily express gratitude and recognize pleasurable experiences in your life for 30 weeks.

Are you NOW! ready to create the habit of expressing gratitude on a daily basis?

Take a bit of time to make a few notes about your intention for using this "Gratitude Journal" or "Pleasure Book" below.

All that we behold is full of blessings.
~ William Wordsworth ~

Monday

Today I was grateful for these experiences or people in my world and what I gave to myself.

Tuesday

Today I was grateful for these experiences or people in my world and what I gave to myself.

Wednesday _____

*Today I was grateful for these experiences or people
in my world and what I gave to myself.*

_____

_____

_____

_____

_____

_____

_____

_____

Thursday _____

*Today I was grateful for these experiences or people
in my world and what I gave to myself.*

_____

_____

_____

_____

_____

_____

_____

_____

Friday

Today I was grateful for these experiences or people in my world and what I gave to myself.

Saturday

Today I was grateful for these experiences or people in my world and what I gave to myself.

Sunday _____

*Today I was grateful for these experiences or people
in my world and what I gave to myself.*

This a wonderful day. I've never seen this one before.
~ Maya Angelou ~

Monday

Today I was grateful for these experiences or people in my world and what I gave to myself.

Tuesday

Today I was grateful for these experiences or people in my world and what I gave to myself.

Wednesday

*Today I was grateful for these experiences or people
in my world and what I gave to myself.*

_____
_____
_____
_____
_____
_____
_____
_____

Thursday

*Today I was grateful for these experiences or people
in my world and what I gave to myself.*

_____
_____
_____
_____
_____
_____
_____
_____

Friday

*Today I was grateful for these experiences or people
in my world and what I gave to myself.*

Saturday

*Today I was grateful for these experiences or people
in my world and what I gave to myself.*

Sunday
Today I was grateful for these experiences or people in my world and what I gave to myself.

Happiness cannot be traveled to, owned, earned, worn or consumed.
Happiness is the spiritual experience of living every minute with love,
grace and gratitude. ~ Denis Waitley ~

Monday

Today I was grateful for these experiences or people
in my world and what I gave to myself.

_____

_____

_____

_____

_____

_____

_____

_____

_____

Tuesday

Today I was grateful for these experiences or people
in my world and what I gave to myself.

_____

_____

_____

_____

_____

_____

_____

_____

Wednesday

Today I was grateful for these experiences or people in my world and what I gave to myself.

Thursday

Today I was grateful for these experiences or people in my world and what I gave to myself.

Friday

*Today I was grateful for these experiences or people
in my world and what I gave to myself.*

Saturday

*Today I was grateful for these experiences or people
in my world and what I gave to myself.*

Sunday ⸻
*Today I was grateful for these experiences or people
in my world and what I gave to myself.*

Joy is a heart full and a mind purified by gratitude.
~ Marietta McCarty ~

Monday

*Today I was grateful for these experiences or people
in my world and what I gave to myself.*

Tuesday

*Today I was grateful for these experiences or people
in my world and what I gave to myself.*

Wednesday _____

*Today I was grateful for these experiences or people
in my world and what I gave to myself.*

_____

_____

_____

_____

_____

_____

_____

_____

Thursday _____

*Today I was grateful for these experiences or people
in my world and what I gave to myself.*

_____

_____

_____

_____

_____

_____

_____

_____

Friday

*Today I was grateful for these experiences or people
in my world and what I gave to myself.*

Saturday

*Today I was grateful for these experiences or people
in my world and what I gave to myself.*

Sunday
Today I was grateful for these experiences or people in my world and what I gave to myself.

Gratitude turns what we have into enough.
~ Author Unknown ~

Monday

Today I was grateful for these experiences or people in my world and what I gave to myself.

Tuesday

Today I was grateful for these experiences or people in my world and what I gave to myself.

Wednesday

*Today I was grateful for these experiences or people
in my world and what I gave to myself.*

Thursday

*Today I was grateful for these experiences or people
in my world and what I gave to myself.*

Friday

Today I was grateful for these experiences or people in my world and what I gave to myself.

Saturday

Today I was grateful for these experiences or people in my world and what I gave to myself.

Sunday

*Today I was grateful for these experiences or people
in my world and what I gave to myself.*

*Expressing gratitude is a natural state of being and
reminds us that we are all connected.*
~ Valerie Elster ~

Monday

*Today I was grateful for these experiences or people
in my world and what I gave to myself.*

Tuesday

*Today I was grateful for these experiences or people
in my world and what I gave to myself.*

Wednesday

*Today I was grateful for these experiences or people
in my world and what I gave to myself.*

Thursday

*Today I was grateful for these experiences or people
in my world and what I gave to myself.*

Friday

*Today I was grateful for these experiences or people
in my world and what I gave to myself.*

Saturday

*Today I was grateful for these experiences or people
in my world and what I gave to myself.*

Sunday
Today I was grateful for these experiences or people in my world and what I gave to myself.

Monday

Today I was grateful for these experiences or people in my world and what I gave to myself.

_____

_____

_____

_____

_____

_____

_____

_____

Tuesday

Today I was grateful for these experiences or people in my world and what I gave to myself.

_____

_____

_____

_____

_____

_____

_____

_____

Wednesday

Today I was grateful for these experiences or people in my world and what I gave to myself.

Thursday

Today I was grateful for these experiences or people in my world and what I gave to myself.

Friday

*Today I was grateful for these experiences or people
in my world and what I gave to myself.*

Saturday

*Today I was grateful for these experiences or people
in my world and what I gave to myself.*

Sunday

Today I was grateful for these experiences or people in my world and what I gave to myself.

There is nothing better than the encouragement of a good friend.
~ Jean Jacques Rousseau ~

Monday

Today I was grateful for these experiences or people in my world and what I gave to myself.

Tuesday

Today I was grateful for these experiences or people in my world and what I gave to myself.

Wednesday _____

*Today I was grateful for these experiences or people
in my world and what I gave to myself.*

_____

_____

_____

_____

_____

_____

_____

_____

_____

_____

Thursday _____

*Today I was grateful for these experiences or people
in my world and what I gave to myself.*

_____

_____

_____

_____

_____

_____

_____

_____

_____

_____

Friday

*Today I was grateful for these experiences or people
in my world and what I gave to myself.*

Saturday

*Today I was grateful for these experiences or people
in my world and what I gave to myself.*

Sunday
*Today I was grateful for these experiences or people
in my world and what I gave to myself.*

Gratitude is not only the greatest of virtues,
but the parent of all the others.
~ Cicero ~

Monday

Today I was grateful for these experiences or people
in my world and what I gave to myself.

Tuesday

Today I was grateful for these experiences or people
in my world and what I gave to myself.

Wednesday

*Today I was grateful for these experiences or people
in my world and what I gave to myself.*

Thursday

*Today I was grateful for these experiences or people
in my world and what I gave to myself.*

Friday

*Today I was grateful for these experiences or people
in my world and what I gave to myself.*

Saturday

*Today I was grateful for these experiences or people
in my world and what I gave to myself.*

Sunday
*Today I was grateful for these experiences or people
in my world and what I gave to myself.*

Monday

Today I was grateful for these experiences or people in my world and what I gave to myself.

_____

_____

_____

_____

_____

_____

_____

_____

Tuesday

Today I was grateful for these experiences or people in my world and what I gave to myself.

_____

_____

_____

_____

_____

_____

_____

_____

Wednesday

*Today I was grateful for these experiences or people
in my world and what I gave to myself.*

Thursday

*Today I was grateful for these experiences or people
in my world and what I gave to myself.*

Friday

*Today I was grateful for these experiences or people
in my world and what I gave to myself.*

Saturday

*Today I was grateful for these experiences or people
in my world and what I gave to myself.*

Sunday _____

*Today I was grateful for these experiences or people
in my world and what I gave to myself.*

Gratitude can transform common days into thanksgivings,
turn routine jobs into joy, and change ordinary opportunities
into blessings. ~ William Arthur Ward ~

Monday

Today I was grateful for these experiences or people
in my world and what I gave to myself.

Tuesday

Today I was grateful for these experiences or people
in my world and what I gave to myself.

Wednesday

Today I was grateful for these experiences or people in my world and what I gave to myself.

Thursday

Today I was grateful for these experiences or people in my world and what I gave to myself.

Friday

Today I was grateful for these experiences or people in my world and what I gave to myself.

Saturday

Today I was grateful for these experiences or people in my world and what I gave to myself.

Sunday

Today I was grateful for these experiences or people in my world and what I gave to myself.

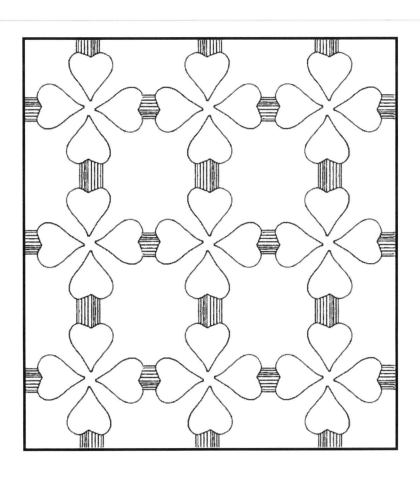

Among the things you can give and still keep are your word,
a smile, and a grateful heart.
~ Zig Ziglar ~

Monday

Today I was grateful for these experiences or people
in my world and what I gave to myself.

Tuesday

Today I was grateful for these experiences or people
in my world and what I gave to myself.

Wednesday ....

*Today I was grateful for these experiences or people
in my world and what I gave to myself.*

_____

_____

_____

_____

_____

_____

_____

_____

Thursday ....

*Today I was grateful for these experiences or people
in my world and what I gave to myself.*

_____

_____

_____

_____

_____

_____

_____

_____

_____

Friday

*Today I was grateful for these experiences or people
in my world and what I gave to myself.*

Saturday

*Today I was grateful for these experiences or people
in my world and what I gave to myself.*

Sunday ....

Today I was grateful for these experiences or people in my world and what I gave to myself.

*Let us be grateful to people who make us happy; they are the
charming gardeners who make our souls blossom.*
~ Marcel Proust ~

Monday

*Today I was grateful for these experiences or people
in my world and what I gave to myself.*

Tuesday

*Today I was grateful for these experiences or people
in my world and what I gave to myself.*

Wednesday

*Today I was grateful for these experiences or people
in my world and what I gave to myself.*

Thursday

*Today I was grateful for these experiences or people
in my world and what I gave to myself.*

Friday _____

*Today I was grateful for these experiences or people
in my world and what I gave to myself.*

Saturday _____

*Today I was grateful for these experiences or people
in my world and what I gave to myself.*

Sunday

Today I was grateful for these experiences or people in my world and what I gave to myself.

We often take for granted the very things
that most deserve our gratitude.
~ Cynthia Ozick ~

Monday

Today I was grateful for these experiences or people
in my world and what I gave to myself.

Tuesday

Today I was grateful for these experiences or people
in my world and what I gave to myself.

Wednesday _____

*Today I was grateful for these experiences or people
in my world and what I gave to myself.*

_____

_____

_____

_____

_____

_____

_____

_____

_____

Thursday _____

*Today I was grateful for these experiences or people
in my world and what I gave to myself.*

_____

_____

_____

_____

_____

_____

_____

_____

Friday _____

Today I was grateful for these experiences or people
in my world and what I gave to myself.

Saturday _____

Today I was grateful for these experiences or people
in my world and what I gave to myself.

Sunday
*Today I was grateful for these experiences or people
in my world and what I gave to myself.*

There are only two ways to live your life. One is as though nothing is a miracle. The other is as though everything is a miracle.
~ Albert Einstein ~

Monday _____

Today I was grateful for these experiences or people in my world and what I gave to myself.

_____

_____

_____

_____

_____

_____

_____

_____

Tuesday _____

Today I was grateful for these experiences or people in my world and what I gave to myself.

_____

_____

_____

_____

_____

_____

_____

_____

Wednesday

Today I was grateful for these experiences or people in my world and what I gave to myself.

Thursday

Today I was grateful for these experiences or people in my world and what I gave to myself.

Friday
*Today I was grateful for these experiences or people
in my world and what I gave to myself.*

Saturday
*Today I was grateful for these experiences or people
in my world and what I gave to myself.*

Sunday

Today I was grateful for these experiences or people in my world and what I gave to myself.

When eating bamboo sprouts, remember the man who planted them.
~ Chinese Proverb ~

Monday

*Today I was grateful for these experiences or people
in my world and what I gave to myself.*

Tuesday

*Today I was grateful for these experiences or people
in my world and what I gave to myself.*

Wednesday

*Today I was grateful for these experiences or people
in my world and what I gave to myself.*

Thursday

*Today I was grateful for these experiences or people
in my world and what I gave to myself.*

Friday

*Today I was grateful for these experiences or people
in my world and what I gave to myself.*

Saturday

*Today I was grateful for these experiences or people
in my world and what I gave to myself.*

Sunday
Today I was grateful for these experiences or people
in my world and what I gave to myself.

No duty is more urgent than that of returning thanks.
~ Unknown ~

Monday

Today I was grateful for these experiences or people in my world and what I gave to myself.

Tuesday

Today I was grateful for these experiences or people in my world and what I gave to myself.

Wednesday

*Today I was grateful for these experiences or people
in my world and what I gave to myself.*

Thursday

*Today I was grateful for these experiences or people
in my world and what I gave to myself.*

Friday _____

Today I was grateful for these experiences or people in my world and what I gave to myself.

Saturday _____

Today I was grateful for these experiences or people in my world and what I gave to myself.

Sunday

*Today I was grateful for these experiences or people
in my world and what I gave to myself.*

You cannot do a kindness too soon because
you never know how soon it will be too late.
~ Ralph Waldo Emerson ~

Monday

*Today I was grateful for these experiences or people
in my world and what I gave to myself.*

Tuesday

*Today I was grateful for these experiences or people
in my world and what I gave to myself.*

Wednesday

*Today I was grateful for these experiences or people
in my world and what I gave to myself.*

Thursday

*Today I was grateful for these experiences or people
in my world and what I gave to myself.*

Friday _____

Today I was grateful for these experiences or people in my world and what I gave to myself.

_____

_____

_____

_____

_____

_____

_____

_____

_____

Saturday _____

Today I was grateful for these experiences or people in my world and what I gave to myself.

_____

_____

_____

_____

_____

_____

_____

_____

_____

Sunday
*Today I was grateful for these experiences or people
in my world and what I gave to myself.*

Real life isn't always going to be perfect or go our way, but the recurring acknowledgement of what is working in our lives can help us not only to survive but surmount our difficulties. ~ Sarah Ban Breathnach ~

Monday

Today I was grateful for these experiences or people in my world and what I gave to myself.

Tuesday

Today I was grateful for these experiences or people in my world and what I gave to myself.

Wednesday

*Today I was grateful for these experiences or people
in my world and what I gave to myself.*

Thursday

*Today I was grateful for these experiences or people
in my world and what I gave to myself.*

Friday

*Today I was grateful for these experiences or people
in my world and what I gave to myself.*

Saturday

*Today I was grateful for these experiences or people
in my world and what I gave to myself.*

Sunday

*Today I was grateful for these experiences or people
in my world and what I gave to myself.*

Some people are always complaining because roses have thorns.
I am thankful that thorns have roses.
~ Alphonse Karr ~

Monday

Today I was grateful for these experiences or people in my world and what I gave to myself.

Tuesday

Today I was grateful for these experiences or people in my world and what I gave to myself.

Wednesday

*Today I was grateful for these experiences or people
in my world and what I gave to myself.*

Thursday

*Today I was grateful for these experiences or people
in my world and what I gave to myself.*

Friday

Today I was grateful for these experiences or people in my world and what I gave to myself.

Saturday

Today I was grateful for these experiences or people in my world and what I gave to myself.

Sunday

Today I was grateful for these experiences or people in my world and what I gave to myself.

Gratitude is a vaccine, an antitoxin, and an antiseptic.
~ John Henry Jowett ~

Monday

*Today I was grateful for these experiences or people
in my world and what I gave to myself.*

Tuesday

*Today I was grateful for these experiences or people
in my world and what I gave to myself.*

Wednesday

Today I was grateful for these experiences or people in my world and what I gave to myself.

Thursday

Today I was grateful for these experiences or people in my world and what I gave to myself.

Friday _____

*Today I was grateful for these experiences or people
in my world and what I gave to myself.*

Saturday _____

*Today I was grateful for these experiences or people
in my world and what I gave to myself.*

Sunday

Today I was grateful for these experiences or people in my world and what I gave to myself.

Give thanks for a little and you will find a lot.
~ The Hausa of Nigeria ~

Monday

*Today I was grateful for these experiences or people
in my world and what I gave to myself.*

Tuesday

*Today I was grateful for these experiences or people
in my world and what I gave to myself.*

Wednesday

Today I was grateful for these experiences or people in my world and what I gave to myself.

Thursday

Today I was grateful for these experiences or people in my world and what I gave to myself.

108

Friday

*Today I was grateful for these experiences or people
in my world and what I gave to myself.*

Saturday

*Today I was grateful for these experiences or people
in my world and what I gave to myself.*

Sunday
*Today I was grateful for these experiences or people
in my world and what I gave to myself.*

Gratitude is riches. Complaint is poverty.
~ Doris Day ~

Monday

Today I was grateful for these experiences or people in my world and what I gave to myself.

Tuesday

Today I was grateful for these experiences or people in my world and what I gave to myself.

Wednesday

*Today I was grateful for these experiences or people
in my world and what I gave to myself.*

Thursday

*Today I was grateful for these experiences or people
in my world and what I gave to myself.*

Friday
*Today I was grateful for these experiences or people
in my world and what I gave to myself.*

Saturday
*Today I was grateful for these experiences or people
in my world and what I gave to myself.*

Sunday

*Today I was grateful for these experiences or people
in my world and what I gave to myself.*

When I started counting my blessings,
my whole life turned around.
~ Willie Nelson ~

Monday

Today I was grateful for these experiences or people
in my world and what I gave to myself.

Tuesday

Today I was grateful for these experiences or people
in my world and what I gave to myself.

Wednesday

*Today I was grateful for these experiences or people
in my world and what I gave to myself.*

Thursday

*Today I was grateful for these experiences or people
in my world and what I gave to myself.*

Friday _____

*Today I was grateful for these experiences or people
in my world and what I gave to myself.*

_____

_____

_____

_____

_____

_____

_____

_____

_____

_____

Saturday _____

*Today I was grateful for these experiences or people
in my world and what I gave to myself.*

_____

_____

_____

_____

_____

_____

_____

_____

_____

_____

Sunday
Today I was grateful for these experiences or people
in my world and what I gave to myself.

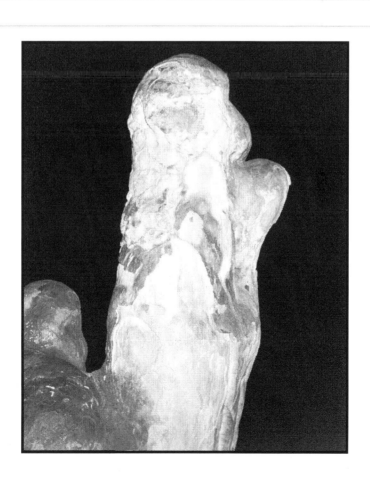

Acknowledging the good that you already have in your life
is the foundation for all abundance.
~ Eckhart Tolle ~

Monday

*Today I was grateful for these experiences or people
in my world and what I gave to myself.*

Tuesday

*Today I was grateful for these experiences or people
in my world and what I gave to myself.*

Wednesday

*Today I was grateful for these experiences or people
in my world and what I gave to myself.*

Thursday

*Today I was grateful for these experiences or people
in my world and what I gave to myself.*

Friday

Today I was grateful for these experiences or people in my world and what I gave to myself.

Saturday

Today I was grateful for these experiences or people in my world and what I gave to myself.

Sunday

*Today I was grateful for these experiences or people
in my world and what I gave to myself.*

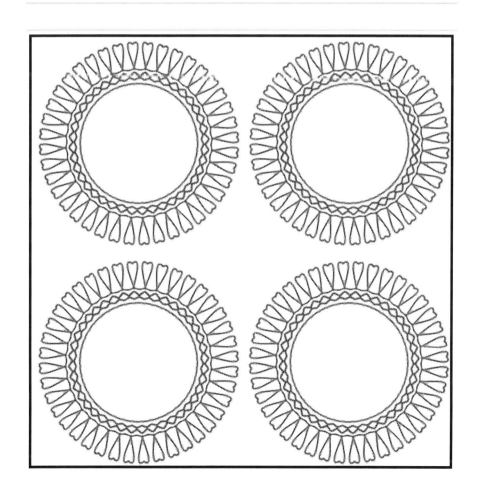

*Gratitude is a quality similar to electricity: it must be produced
and discharged and used up in order to exist at all.*
~ William Faulkner ~

Monday

*Today I was grateful for these experiences or people
in my world and what I gave to myself.*

Tuesday

*Today I was grateful for these experiences or people
in my world and what I gave to myself.*

Wednesday _____

Today I was grateful for these experiences or people in my world and what I gave to myself.

_____

Thursday _____

Today I was grateful for these experiences or people in my world and what I gave to myself.

_____

Friday _____

*Today I was grateful for these experiences or people
in my world and what I gave to myself.*

_____

_____

_____

_____

_____

_____

_____

_____

Saturday _____

*Today I was grateful for these experiences or people
in my world and what I gave to myself.*

_____

_____

_____

_____

_____

_____

_____

_____

Sunday
Today I was grateful for these experiences or people in my world and what I gave to myself.

I never get tired of the blue sky.
~ Vincent Van Gogh ~

Monday _____

*Today I was grateful for these experiences or people
in my world and what I gave to myself.*

Tuesday _____

*Today I was grateful for these experiences or people
in my world and what I gave to myself.*

Wednesday _____

Today I was grateful for these experiences or people in my world and what I gave to myself.

_____

_____

_____

_____

_____

_____

_____

_____

Thursday _____

Today I was grateful for these experiences or people in my world and what I gave to myself.

_____

_____

_____

_____

_____

_____

_____

_____

Friday _____

*Today I was grateful for these experiences or people
in my world and what I gave to myself.*

_____
_____
_____
_____
_____
_____
_____
_____
_____
_____

Saturday _____

*Today I was grateful for these experiences or people
in my world and what I gave to myself.*

_____
_____
_____
_____
_____
_____
_____
_____
_____
_____

Sunday

*Today I was grateful for these experiences or people
in my world and what I gave to myself.*

The body heals with play,
The mind heals with laughter
And the spirit heals with joy. ~ Proverb

Monday

Today I was grateful for these experiences or people in my world and what I gave to myself.

Tuesday

Today I was grateful for these experiences or people in my world and what I gave to myself.

Wednesday

*Today I was grateful for these experiences or people
in my world and what I gave to myself.*

Thursday

*Today I was grateful for these experiences or people
in my world and what I gave to myself.*

Friday

Today I was grateful for these experiences or people in my world and what I gave to myself.

Saturday

Today I was grateful for these experiences or people in my world and what I gave to myself.

Sunday

*Today I was grateful for these experiences or people
in my world and what I gave to myself.*

Courtesies of a small and trivial character are the ones which strike deepest in the grateful and appreciating heart.
~ Henry Clay ~

Monday

Today I was grateful for these experiences or people in my world and what I gave to myself.

Tuesday

Today I was grateful for these experiences or people in my world and what I gave to myself.

Wednesday _____

*Today I was grateful for these experiences or people
in my world and what I gave to myself.*

_____
_____
_____
_____
_____
_____
_____
_____
_____

Thursday _____

*Today I was grateful for these experiences or people
in my world and what I gave to myself.*

_____
_____
_____
_____
_____
_____
_____
_____
_____

Friday _____
Today I was grateful for these experiences or people in my world and what I gave to myself.

Saturday _____
Today I was grateful for these experiences or people in my world and what I gave to myself.

Sunday

*Today I was grateful for these experiences or people
in my world and what I gave to myself.*

As each day comes to us refreshed and anew, so does my gratitude renew itself daily. The breaking of the sun over the horizon is my grateful heart dawning upon a blessed world. ~ Adabella Radici ~

Monday

Today I was grateful for these experiences or people in my world and what I gave to myself.

_____

_____

_____

_____

_____

_____

_____

_____

_____

Tuesday

Today I was grateful for these experiences or people in my world and what I gave to myself.

_____

_____

_____

_____

_____

_____

_____

_____

_____

Wednesday

Today I was grateful for these experiences or people
in my world and what I gave to myself.

Thursday

Today I was grateful for these experiences or people
in my world and what I gave to myself.

140

Friday

*Today I was grateful for these experiences or people
in my world and what I gave to myself.*

Saturday

*Today I was grateful for these experiences or people
in my world and what I gave to myself.*

Sunday

*Today I was grateful for these experiences or people
in my world and what I gave to myself.*

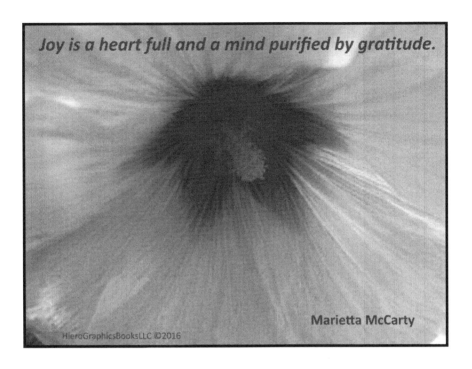

Joy is a heart full and a mind purified by gratitude.

Marietta McCarty

There is nothing better than the encouragement of a good friend.

Jean Jacques Rousseau

If you haven't already downloaded your free bonus Gratitude Cards, do it NOW!

You can sign up to download,
"36 Gratitude Quote Cards", **at:**

www.hierographicsbooksllc.com/quote-cards-gratitude-journal.

On the left page are a couple of samples of the cards you will get when you download the pdf file of the for your 36 Gratitude Quote Cards.

THANK YOU!

FOR PURCHASING
THIS GRATITUDE JOURNAL.

EXPRESSING YOUR GRATITUDE AND ACKNOWLEDGING THE PLEASURABLE THINGS IN YOUR WORLD DAILY IS THE BEST WAY TO CREATE YOUR NEW MORE HOLISTIC AND JOYFUL LIFE.

Made in the USA
Columbia, SC
08 February 2019